Text: *Dennis Kelsall*
Series editor: *Tony Bowerman*
Photographs: *Dennis Kelsall, Paul Newcombe/ www.paulnewcombephotography.co.uk, James Grant/www.jamesgphotography.co.uk, Steve Foster, Steve Wood, Tony Bowerman, Shutterstock, Dreamstime, Fotolia*

Design: *Carl Rogers*

N Northern
E Eye

Northern Eye Books

ISBN 978-1-908632-04-3

A CIP catalogue record for this book is available from the British Library.

www.northerneyebooks.co.uk

Cover: *Gritstone stacks on Kinder Edge (Walk 1)*
Photo: Paul Newcombe
www.paulnewcombephotography.co.uk

First published in 2013 by

Northern Eye Books Limited

Northern Eye Books, Tattenhall, Cheshire CH3 9PX

Email: tony@northerneyebooks.com

For sales enquiries, please call 01928 723 744

Contents

England's first National Park

CREATED IN 1951, THE PEAK DISTRICT NATIONAL PARK extends over six counties and is the second most visited of Britain's National Parks. Its highest point lies upon the seemingly remote Kinder plateau, where a mass trespass in 1932 marked the turning point in a long and sometimes bitter campaign that led to the creation of Britain's National Parks and the open access we enjoy today.

The high, peaty moorlands of the northern Dark Peak are founded on gritstone, their stark grandeur accentuated by impressive weatherworn tors and edges. The moors extend out of the Pennines in two horns that enclose the limestone plateau of the White Peak, an upland pasture cleft by narrow gorges and dales. The transition between the two is startlingly abrupt and each has a distinctive character and beauty all its own; the wild openness of the north contrasting with a more intimate southern landscape dotted with small villages and criss-crossed by old lanes.

A panoramic view over Ladybower Reservoir from Win Hill

Moors and Tors

The uplands of the Peak bear the characteristics of hills rather than mountains: high, undulating plateaux dissected by deep, meandering valleys. Yet there is little uniformity; the seemingly remote moorland of the Kinder plateau is in sharp contrast to the gentler and lower upland heaths found farther south.

These landscapes change subtly with the seasons and, for those who care to look, are rich in wildlife. There are birds, hares, and foxes; and in summer, adders and lizards bask in the sun, while butterflies dance in the remotest places.

> "A great rolling moor. Except for a few moor farmers, the plover and the curlew are the only inhabitants …"

The Adventure of the Priory School, Sir Arthur Conan Doyle, 1903

TOP 10 **Walks:** Moors & Tors

MOST OF THE PEAK'S UPLAND MOOR is largely pathless and the higher reaches are usually attainable only by a long and strenuous walk. Nevertheless, many of the most atmospheric and spectacular spots can be reached with relative ease and reflect the special qualities for which the more remote spots are justly valued. The walks described here explore their infinitely varying character, seeking out the best viewpoints and revealing magical hidden corners.

The edge of Kinder — page 8

The Wool Packs — page 14

Lose Hill & Mam Tor — page 20

Win Hill — page 26

Looking into Edale from the edge of the Kinder plateau

Onto the edge of Kinder

A strenuous walk from the valley onto the rim of the Kinder plateau with grand views

What to expect:

Long, steady climb on field and rugged moorland paths, returning along a good track

Distance/time: 10.5km/ 6½ miles. Allow 3½ hours

Start: Bowden Bridge pay and display car park

Grid ref: SK 048 869

Ordnance Survey Map: Explorer OL1 *The Peak District: Dark Peak area: Kinder Scout, Bleaklow, Black Hill & Ladybower Reservoir*

After the Walk: The Sportsman Inn, 400 metres/ ¼ mile west of Bowden Bridge car park

Walk outline

After following a lane and track to Tunstead Clough Farm, the way takes to the fields to reach the foot of Kinderlow End. A clear moorland path then rises across Kinder Low's steep flank, eventually broaching the edge beside the Red Brook gully. With the hard work over, it is an enjoyable ramble over Kinder Low and down to Edale Cross, from where a packhorse track leads back into the valley.

Kinder

Kinder Scout will forever be remembered by ramblers for a mass trespass in 1932. Some 500 members of Manchester and Sheffield walking clubs rallied on the hill to protest the injustice of being denied lawful access to England's open country. Although neither the first nor the last, the size of the gathering and the harshness of punishment meted out made the trespass a turning point in the campaign and eventually led to the enactment of The National Parks and Access to the Countryside Act in 1949. The Peak District National Park was the first to be created in 1951, and a plaque was later placed in the Bowden Bridge car park to commemorate the Trespass.

Barn below Kinder

Red grouse

The Walk

1. Take the lane opposite the car park entrance, which crosses the **River Sett** and then swings left in front of the **Hayfield Camping and Caravanning Club site**. The lane bends again at the river's confluence with the **Kinder**, which is spanned by an old packhorse bridge, known locally as the **Roman Bridge**. Carry on beside the Sett to the next bridge. Cross, but just before a second bridge, leave ahead through a gate along a metalled track to 'Kinderstones and Tunstead House'.

2. After a sharp right-hand bend and bridge, bear right at a fork, the track winding past a cottage and **Tunstead House** to a gate and stile. Walk forward at the field edge and then bear slightly right across the next field. Keep climbing across successive fields towards the prominent bluff of Kinderlow End,

eventually passing through a couple of gates onto the open moor. Go left to a final gate and stile at the foot of **Kinderlow End**.

Stone field barns, remote from the main farm became a feature of hillside pastures during the 18th century, assisting farmers to overwinter herds of cattle. Hay harvested during the summer was stored in an upper loft, the stalls below providing shelter from the elements for the animals.

3. Keep straight ahead, a clear path developing that gently climbs across the flank of the hill. Beyond a stream gully, the path becomes more rugged, wandering between the scattered

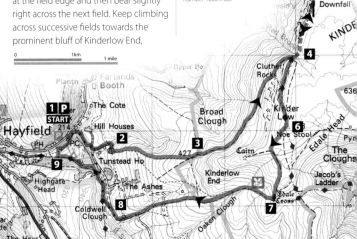

Stone sentinels: *Eroded gritstone rocks frame distant views over Edale*

boulders of **Cluther Rocks** for another 800 metres/½ mile. Approaching the gully of **Red Brook** (SK 078 879), watch for the path bearing off to the right to emerge onto the top of the edge beside the head of Red Brook. Should you miss it, the onward path soon narrows and turns in to meet the stream lower down the gully. Although there is an easy scramble out on the far bank, the best course is to retrace your steps to find the proper path.

(The top of the **Kinder Downfall** [**5**] lies some 800 metres/½ mile north along the path to the left and is worth a detour if you have time to spare.)

4. Otherwise turn right, shortly reaching a cairn. (To the left a rough trod picks across the moss towards Point 636, the highest point of **Kinder Scout**. Although it lies only 800 metres/½ mile away, the terrain is demanding and the detour is inadvisable in poor weather or for those without excellent navigation skills.)

The main path continues ahead past more cairns, shortly levelling to reveal

Kinder garden: *Dramatic gritsone stacks decorate the edge of Kinder Scout*

the **Kinder Low 'trig' column** perched upon a large boulder over to the left.

6. From the trig, head south of west to regain the main path beside a large cairn. Follow it away, gently losing height to a fork by another cairn. Take the left branch, which soon becomes flagged and leads to a second fork. Again keep left, the way gradually descending towards the hillock of **Swine's Back**. The path passes it on the right to join a wall, following that down to emerge through a gate onto a broad track at **Edale Cross**.

7. Follow the track right through a gate, just beyond which you will see the cross, tucked away in a small alcove to the right. An old packhorse route, the track leads off the hill, later becoming metalled and eventually reaching a junction. Keep ahead, passing a farm and shortly arriving at a fork.

8. Pass through the lefthand gate, marked 'Horses and Cycles', crossing a stream to follow a rising track above a beech wood. Carry on to the crest of the hill, where the **Pennine Bridleway** joins from the left. A few metres farther along, bear left onto a rough track signed to 'Hayfield'. The way soon levels,

running to a gate at the edge of a wood. Immediately beyond, take the right fork and descend at the edge of the trees. Ignore a stile beside **Stones House** and continue down to a crossing footpath from Elle Bank.

9. Follow it over a stile on the right, dropping to a **campsite**. Through consecutive gates, cross its drive and then turn right on a riverside path that leads up to **Bowden Bridge** beside the car park to complete the walk. ♦

Edale Cross

Thought to have been erected originally by Cistercian monks from Basingwerk Abbey in the 12th century, Edale Cross marks the junction of the old parish wards of Glossop, Hopedale and Longdendale. Discovered fallen and buried in the peat, it was re-erected in 1810 by five forward-thinking local farmers, whose carved initials it now bears.

The Wool Packs lit by the first rays of the sun

The Wool Packs

A strenuous walk to explore weatherworn outcrops on the edge of the Kinder plateau

What to expect:
A long climb on rugged hill paths with several stream crossings, returning along a good track

Distance/time: 9km/ 5½ miles. Allow 3 hours

Start: Barber Booth car park

Grid ref: SK 107 847

Ordnance Survey Map: Explorer OL1 *The Peak District: Dark Peak area: Kinder Scout, Bleaklow, Black Hill & Ladybower Reservoir*

After the Walk: The Rambler Inn or the Old Nag's Head at nearby Edale

Walk outline

The walk begins along a quiet lane to Upper Booth, there entering the pretty, wooded clough of Crowden Brook. Climbing with the stream into the deep upper valley, the way becomes more rugged, eventually clambering onto the edge beneath Crowden Tower. The onward path weaves easily past weather-sculpted crags and rocks before turning downhill to a steep track descending Jacob's Ladder. It is then an undemanding stroll back to the car park.

Strange stones

The Wool Packs

Taking their name from the fact that some of the weatherworn boulders resemble the bales of wool once carried to market on the backs of packhorses, the Wool Packs are part of a group of intriguing rocky outcrops that fringe the high Kinder plateau. Crowden Tower, Pym Chair and Noe Stool are other features named on the map, although a fertile imagination will see many more shapes in these mysterious formations. The wider scenery is impressive too, with expansive views across the Vale of Edale to Brown Knoll, the long Mam Tor ridge and the deep clefts that bite far into the hillside.

Moorland bilberries

The Walk

1. Continue up the lane from the **Barber Booth car park**, winding right and then left to cross the infant **River Noe**. Beyond the bus turning circle at **Upper Booth**, the way degrades to a track and drops to a bridge at the foot of Crowden Brook.

2. Immediately after the bridge, leave through a wicket gate on the right and follow a path above **Crowden Brook** up the wooded clough. Eventually, just beyond a barn, cross a stile and continue at the edge of pasture. Towards the top of the field, watch for the path dropping back to the river. Over a **plank bridge**,

climb to a gate and follow the path left to another gate.

3. A final gate takes the way into the wild upper valley, much of which, like the plateau above, is cared for by the National Trust. Progressing into the narrowing gorge, pause to look back for the view across the valley. Before long the path falls beside the stream, becoming increasingly rugged as it picks a course between the boulders.

Although rocky, the ongoing route is clear, occasionally crossing and re-crossing the flow. The path eventually settles on the western flank and then gives up with the stream to rise energetically along the valley

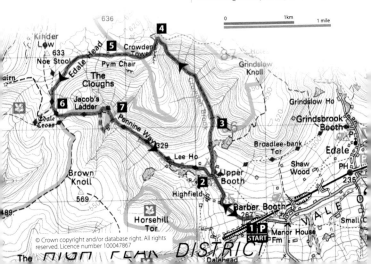

Rocky road?: *Weatherworn boulders litter the open moorland into the far distance*

side towards boulders at the foot of **Crowden Tower**, the imposing crag dominating the gorge. A stiff pull leads to a crossing path. Turn right to the head of the valley, where the stream tumbles from the edge.

4. Climb steeply left past a great canted slab, beyond which the path gains the top of **Crowden Tower**. The ongoing route lies clear across the sloping moorland fringe of the plateau, winding between outcrops and boulders of millstone grit that ice, water and wind have fashioned into weird and wonderful shapes.

Mythical creatures and anthropomorphic forms sprout from the ground, some reminiscent of the ancient idols of Easter Island or Mexico. The natural shapes have influenced modern artists; the famous sculptor Henry Moore wandered amongst the boulders here seeking inspiration for his work.

Gazing beyond the rocks, the view stretches across the Vale of Edale to Rushup Edge, Mam Tor and the Great Ridge.

Sun and shadow: *The view back down Crowden Clough from the Wool Packs*

5. Beyond **Pym Chair**, the path becomes intermittently flagged. Reaching a large cairn, bear left at a vague fork, passing **Noe Stool** and gently descending towards the distant Swine's Back. Continue ahead at a second large cairn, where the **Pennine Way** joins from Kinder Low.

6. At a fork below **Swine's Back**, bear left onto a descending stepped path. Keep left at another split, eventually dropping to a large cairn at the head of **Jacob's Ladder**.

The path again branches, but either will do; that ahead dropping steeply while the one on the right takes an easier zigzag line. Both meet at a narrow **packhorse bridge** spanning the **River Noe** at the bottom.

The narrow stone bridge across the Noe lies on a medieval trail that climbed over the pass between Edale and Hayfield. Led by jaggers, teams of laden packhorses were the hauliers of their day, porting bales of wool, bags of salt and other commodities between the towns and villages. Numerous bridges such as this took them safely across streams that could flood dangerously after rain. The bridge is named after a local

17th-century farmer, Jacob Marshall, who built the steep track up the hill.

7. Through a gate, a broad path lopes easily down the valley to **Lee Farm**, where the National Trust has restored one of the barns as an information shelter. Beyond, the way becomes metalled and leads back to **Upper Booth**. Retrace your outward route back to the car park to complete the walk. ♦

The Edale Railway

The hillocks behind the Barber Booth car park are mounds of spoil excavated during the construction of the Cowburn tunnel. The tunnel took the Midland railway from Sheffield out of the head of Edale towards Manchester. Opened in 1894, it was the fourth cross-country railway route over the Pennines. The summit of the line actually lies within the 3,700-yard tunnel, more or less beneath the highest point of the ridge above.

Dawn on the Great Ridge, above Castleton

Lose Hill & Mam Tor

A spectacular and undulating walk on one of the Peak District's most popular ridges

What to expect:
Clear field and moor-land paths with several sustained ascents

Distance/time: 8.5km/ 5¼ miles. Allow 3 hours

Start: Mam Nick National Trust pay and display car park

Grid ref: SK 123 832

Ordnance Survey Map: Explorer OL1 *The Peak District: Dark Peak area: Kinder Scout, Bleaklow, Black Hill & Ladybower Reservoir*

After the Walk: Cafés and pubs in nearby Castleton

Walk outline

The walk begins below the southern flank of the hill. After following the coach road that once led to Castleton, there is then a steady climb to Hollins Cross on the Mam Tor ridge. An undulating path traverses the crest to Lose Hill, broken by a sharp ascent of Back Tor. After returning to Hollins Cross, the route remains with the ridge onto Mam Tor itself, dropping beyond the summit back to the car park.

The Great Ridge

Stretching for more than 3 kilometres/2 miles, the Great Ridge separates the Vale of Edale from the head of the Hope Valley and offers some of the finest views in the Peak District National Park.

Ladder stile

Mam Tor's highest point was the site of a Bronze and Iron Age settlement, whose impressive embanked defences are still clearly visible from afar. Lose Hill, the eastern culmination of the ridge, is otherwise known as Ward's Piece, and was bought by the Ramblers and gifted to the Labour politician GBH Ward in recognition of his campaigning work to secure public access to open country. He subsequently gave the land to the National Trust.

Wheatear

The Walk

1. Exiting the car park, follow the main road left, crossing to a lay-by a few metres along. Leave through a gate just beyond and then fork left on a field trod across **Windy Knoll**.

Emerging onto the road at the far side, go left, but then turn off right along a narrow lane to the **Blue John Cavern**. Pass through a gate at the end of the lane and pick your way carefully through the debris of an abandoned road.

2. At the bottom, pass through a second gate and take the track ahead towards **Mam Farm**. Almost immediately, leave through a wicket gate on the left, from which a rising grass path angles across the sweeping hillside.

Remain with the lower path where it shortly forks, contouring above **Mam Farm**. Keep going over a stile, the way later joined by a second path from below as it approaches a gap in a wall. Beyond another gate, the gradient steepens for the final pull to the ridge at **Hollins Cross**, where a view suddenly opens across the Vale of Edale to the massive bulk of Kinder Scout.

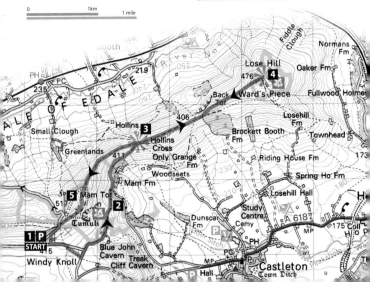

Summit sunrise: *Dawn lights up the Ordnance Survey 'trig' point on Mam Tor*

3. Follow the ridge path to the right, undulating easily over **Barker Bank** to the foot of **Back Tor**. There, mount a stile and climb the stepped path to the top of the impressive outcrop.

Beyond, the ridge falls before a gentle pull onto **Lose Hill**, where a viewing table helps identify the surrounding landmarks.

This is a good place to look out for wheatears. These summer visitors from sub-Saharan Africa arrive to breed on open uplands where larvae and insects provide abundant food. Habitually fluttering ahead from perch to perch as you approach and a black 'T' on the tail are pointers to their identification. They also have a light rump, from which their old name of 'white arse' is derived.

4. Retrace your steps to **Hollins Cross**, but now continue along the curving ridge, steadily climbing towards the **summit of Mam Tor**.

Mam Tor is known locally as the Shivering Mountain, its southern face slumping

Morning has broken: *First light illuminates dawn mists rising below the Great Ridge*

in a massive rotational landslide that began more than 4,000 years ago. The over-steepened slope was created during the last glacial period, and the ongoing movement is sustained by water seeping through the layers of sand and mudstone.

Part of the main route between Manchester and Sheffield, the road at its foot was built in 1819 by the Sheffield Turnpike Company. However, continual repairs were required until massive landslides in 1974 and 1977 finally brought home the futility of keeping it open. Over the years since its construction the road

has been displaced by over 40 metres, the broken remains a graphic demonstration of the forces of nature.

Approaching the top, the path passes through the prehistoric defensive ramparts of **Mam Tor hillfort**, the way then levelling to reach the Ordnance Survey 'trig' point.

The Mam Tor 'trig' point stands on the site of a Bronze Age tumulus, underlining the ancient importance of the area to early British settlers. A warmer, drier climate made these hills ideal for agriculture and, right through to the Iron Age high ground was often a favoured site for settlement. Excavation has shown that the timber

palisade originally topping the still-impressive defensive ramparts was later replaced in stone and within the enclosure numerous hut circles have been identified, all suggesting that this was an Iron Age village of importance.

5. The path carries on over the top, steeply losing height to a gate onto the lane at **Mam Nick**. Walk forward but then branch left, taking a descending path through trees back to the car park to complete the walk. ♦

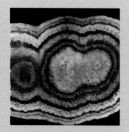

Blue John

Blue John is a rare form of fluorspar, prized for the blue-yellow colouring of its crystals. It was first mined in Castleton by the Romans, and two vases turned from the stone were discovered at Pompeii. Blue John became popular during the eighteenth century, and was often used for ornaments and as decoration on marble fireplaces. Mining still continues on a small scale and today the strange blue stone is fashioned into jewellery.

Ladybower Reservoir: one of the overflow wells

Win Hill

A short but energetic walk to a fine viewpoint above the Ladybower Reservoir

What to expect:
Long, sometimes steep climb on woodland paths; leisurely descent to reservoir

Distance/time: 7km/ 4¼ miles. Allow 2½ hours

Start: Heatherdene pay and display car park, Ladybower

Grid ref: SK 202 859

Ordnance Survey Map: Explorer OL1 *The Peak District: Dark Peak area: Kinder Scout, Bleaklow, Black Hill & Ladybower Reservoir*

After the Walk: The Ladybower Inn at Bamford, on the A57 Sheffield-Manchester road

Walk outline

A wooded trail connects the car park with the Ladybower Dam over which the walk passes to reach the forested slopes of Win Hill. A good path takes the onward way through the trees cloaking its lower flank, breaking onto open moor for a final sharp pull onto the summit. Continuing over the top, the route drops back across heather to the north and eventually descends through the plantation to regain the shore of the lake.

Win Hill

Although not particularly high, Win Hill occupies the end of a long, thin tail that extends from the Kinder plateau to separate the rivers Noe and Hope from the Ashop and Derwent. The ground falls away steeply on three sides, while the summit of the hill rises some 120 metres above the ridge to make it a distinctive landmark from miles around.

Easily reached from the villages surrounding its foot, it is a favourite place from which to watch a summer sunset, although if you don't know the area well, don't linger too long for the woodland paths can become quickly dark.

Summit of Win Hill

Crossbill

The Walk

1. Leave the car park past the toilets to follow a path south through the trees. After a good 400 metres/¼ mile it drops to a **monument** beside the road that commemorates the opening of the reservoir. Cross and continue through gates along the top of the **dam**. On the far side, turn right along the service drive, walking some 250 metres to find a track delving into the trees.

2. Signed to 'New Barn', it angles up the hillside, soon levelling through a gate into a clearing to meet a broader crossing track. To the left it rises more gently across the slope of the hill, occasional waymarks directing you along the main track. After 800 metres/½

mile, the track levels to a junction above **Parkin Clough**.

3. Turn right to climb a steep and intermittently stepped path beside a brook. At the top, pass through a gate to a crossing of paths. The way lies ahead, signed inevitably upwards through the thinning upper fringe of the forest. Eventually leaving the trees behind, the path continues through a gap in the wall to attack the final leg of the ascent across an open, heathery hillside to the **summit of Win Hill**.

4. Carry on past the **summit 'trig' column** to drop along the western spine of the hill, the gradient soon easing as a path joins from the left. Walk a few metres farther to draw beside a kissing-gate in the lefthand wall.

5. Instead of passing through, turn right on a narrow path that strikes out across the heather, descending below the northern flank of the hill towards the forest boundary which appears in the middle distance. Reaching a crossing of paths, walk ahead through a kissing-gate, the way signed to 'Ladybower'. Beyond a felled area, the path continues through young plantation, soon reaching another gate.

Purple heather and blue water: *Looking down from Win Hill over Ladybower Reservoir*

Now in mature forest, carry on straight down the hill to meet a crossing track. Again keep ahead on a narrowing path, ignoring a broad logger's track off to the left lower down.

6. Eventually meeting a waymarked broad crossing track, turn right. Shortly, you pass through a gate to arrive at a junction of tracks. Take the broad one on the left, heading down once more. Disregard crossing paths until you reach the service drive above the **lake shore** at the bottom. Follow it right back to the **dam** and return to the car park to complete the walk. ♦

Ladybower Reservoir

Hindered by the Second World War, the Ladybower Reservoir took ten years to complete and was opened by King George VI in 1943. The lake flooded the converging valleys of the rivers Ashop and Derwent. At the time, it was the largest reservoir in Britain. Half a century later the dam underwent a massive refurbishment, which included the provision of the pathway across the top of the dam, some 45 metres above the base of the valley.

Looking down on Ladybower Reservoir from Whinstone Lee Tor

Whinstone Lee Tor

Whinstone Lee Tor marks the end of Derwent Edge and is superbly situated for views over the Ladybower Reservoir

What to expect:
Woodland and forest paths; initial steep descent on the return

Distance/time: 6km / 3¾ miles. Allow 2 hours

Start: Roadside parking on the A57 by the eastern end of the Ashopton Viaduct

Grid ref: SK 196 864

Ordnance Survey Map: Explorer OL1 *The Peak District: Dark Peak area: Kinder Scout, Bleaklow, Black Hill & Ladybower Reservoir*

After the Walk: The Ladybower Inn at Bamford, on the A57 Sheffield-Manchester road

Walk outline

The circuit begins along a forestry track that winds up into plantation above the former village of Ashopton. Carrying on, the way gains height through the Ladybower Wood Nature Reserve and then on the flank of an open moor that looks across to the high profile of Stanage Edge on the opposite side of the valley. Doubling back above Cutthroat Bridge, the ascent continues easily across the moor to gain the end of the ridge. The return initially drops steeply from the tor through a rocky gully, but the descent soon becomes more leisurely, first across moor and then through conifer plantation.

Starting out

Whinstone Lee Tor

Revelling in the splendid scenery of the surrounding hills, Whinstone Lee Tor is the final prominence in the long run of the Derwent Edge that has dropped from Back Tor, to the north. The western slopes are cloaked in pine, planted to help purify the water draining into the reservoir below, but the woods to the south east are one of the few remaining upland areas of sessile oak that was once the climax vegetation of the area. As many as 75 varieties of lichen grow among the trees.

Lichen

The Walk

1. Walk from the roadside parking towards the **Ashopton Viaduct**, branching off to the right just before it up a gated service drive. Swing through the sharp right hand bend and carry on beyond the end of the tarmac up a gravel drive.

2. Keep ahead through gates at the top to continue on a path signed to 'Cutthroat Bridge'. After undulating across the steep flank of the hill the path passes behind the **Ladybower Inn** to join a rough track rising from the road. Follow it on up the hill, soon passing through a gate into the **Ladybower Wood Nature Reserve**.

The wood is one of the few remaining upland oak woods in the Peak District and supports summer visitors such as pied flycatchers, wood warblers and tree pipits.

Where the way divides, keep right, later passing out of the reserve to walk across the slope of the moor above **Ladybower Brook**.

3. Approaching **Cutthroat Bridge**, there is a fork in the path. Bear left, passing beneath power cables and curving past the foot of **Highshaw Clough** to join a rising path.

Now heading west, climb from the valley and carry on steadily upwards across the open moor. Broaching the ridge at a junction of paths a superb view suddenly opens out at the summit, which is

A boulder view: *Ladybower Reservoir from the National Trust's Whinstone Lee Tor*

best enjoyed from a small promontory reached by the path straight ahead.

4. Return to the junction and turn sharp left, dropping steeply on a rocky path through a narrow gully. The gradient eases at the bottom, the path curving around to the left through bracken to join a wall. The path continues beside the wall, eventually running at the edge of a conifer plantation. Keep forward as the path enters the trees, eventually emerging through a gate at the head of the track from **Ashopton**. Turn right and follow it back to the main road to complete the walk. ♦

Cutthroat Bridge

The ominous name of Cutthroat Bridge appeared in 1635 after a man was found 'with a wound to his throat' just above it in Highshaw Clough. He died two days later at Bamford Hall, where he had been taken to recover. The name lingered even after the bridge was rebuilt in 1821 and so did its notoriety, for in 2007 a headless corpse was found nearby. Two Sheffield men were subsequently convicted of the crime.

Looking across the fields to the amazing Eldon Hole

Peak Forest & Eldon Hole

A walk over open moors and pastures visiting two of the original 'Seven Wonders of the Peak'

What to expect:
Clear tracks and lane; short section across pathless moorland pasture

Distance/time: 7km/ 4½ miles. Allow 2½ hours

Start: Peak Forest, roadside parking on Church Lane

Grid ref: SK 114 794

Ordnance Survey Map: Explorers OL1 *The Peak District: Dark Peak area: Kinder Scout, Bleaklow, Black Hill & Ladybower Reservoir* AND OL24 *Peak District: White Peak area: Buxton, Bakewell, Matlock & Dovedale*

After the Walk: Devonshire Arms, in Peak Forest village

Walk outline

After taking the lane through Old Dam, the route climbs past Sweet Knoll and on at the edge of the moor to Eldon Hole. The way continues over the eastern end of Eldon Hill to pick up an old highway. The return follows Oxlow Rake, the course of a vein of lead ore, to Oxlow Farm and ends with the lane back into the hamlet.

The Wonders of the Peak

Remote and rumpled in forbidding hills, the Peak was once largely avoided by those without specific reason to visit. The first hints of its 'Wonders' appeared in William Camden's Elizabethan topographical survey of Britain:

> *There are in High Peak wonders three,*
> *A deepe hole, Cave, and Den.*

Echoing the 'Wonders of the Ancient World', later writers took up the theme, establishing a 'Grand Tour' for the adventurous traveller. The list included both the Peak Forest (a Norman royal hunting preserve) and Eldon Hole, a dark gape in the hillside once thought bottomless.

Eldon dew pond

Common blue butterfly

Mother earth: *Old mine spoil heaps on Eldon Hill, with Rushup Edge behind*

The Walk

1. Follow Church Lane to **Old Dam**, the original settlement of **Peak Forest**. Go left at the end in the direction of 'Perryfoot'.

Peak Forest's church was built in 1657 as a private chapel for the Countess of Devonshire. Its chaplain conducted marriages but was not required to record details and so the church, like that at Gretna Green, attracted elopements, a practice that ended only in 1938.

2. After 200 metres, turn off into **Eldon Lane**. Walk up to the end, continuing through the yard of **Eldon Lane Farm**. Beyond a gate at the top, keep with the left wall as it soon swings to the left, bounding the edge of the moor. Carry on through a gate above a strip of woodland towards **Eldon Hole**, now seen ahead on the hillside. Be very careful if you decide to explore within the fenced enclosure: the drop is sheer.

Up close, it is easy to appreciate how the dark chasm of Eldon Hole struck awe and terror into a superstitious people, whose simple way of life followed the seasons and was largely governed by nature. The fathomless gape was deemed the entrance to an underworld, inhabited by demons and spirits. They had the power to bring misfortune upon those who neglected the proper courtesies or intruded upon the other world, and such places were avoided. In the 16th century, a man was lowered down at the end of a rope, but the experience struck terror in his heart and by the time he was hauled up, he had lost his mind and died within a few short days. Exaggerated claims finally imagined its depth at over three miles and a goose thrown down supposedly emerged several days later from the caves at Castleton. It was not until 1780 that the first scientific exploration took place, when John Lloyd ascertained its depth at 70 metres. However, another century passed before John Tym and Rooke Pennington of Castleton

discovered the huge cavern at its foot. Today, Eldon Hole is recognised as the deepest cave system in the Peak and draws potholers from across Europe.

3. With your back to the enclosure gate, walk away to the left across the slope of the hill, above a **dew pond**. Continue up the hillside, making for wooden railings enclosing a **capped lead mine** that soon comes into view. Cresting the hill, maintain the same direction towards the distinctive distant summit of Win Hill.

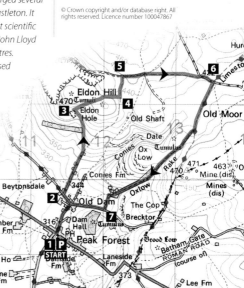

Holey land: *Looking down from the walled fields that surround the curious Eldon Hole*

Descend past the grassed scars of more workings to a bridle gate tucked into the corner where fence and wall meet.

4. A contained path leads away at the field edge, ending through a gate onto a crossing track. Out to the left at the edge of the hill, the stark cliff face is part of the massive **Eldon Hill Quarry**, which was worked for almost 50 years until its eventual closure in 1999.

5. Go right along the track, paralleling old lead workings that followed a vein of ore across the hillside. Keep straight ahead for just over a kilometre/¾ mile until you reach the fourth gate.

6. Go through the gate and immediately leave the track, turning through another gate on the right. Walk away alongside the right-hand wall. At the far end of the enclosure, go into the corner and pass through the gate on the right. The way continues along a walled track beside the extensive **Oxlow Rake workings**, which follow a vein of lead ore for 1.5 kilometres/1 mile across the hill.

Deep trenches and long lines of spoil reveal the extent of lead workings as miners followed rich veins of ore across the hillside.

Beyond the crest, the track falls through a beech wood. Keep ahead past **Oxlow Farm** to emerge over a stile beside the farm's entrance. Now follow a track away to the left.

7. Reaching a junction, walk right down the hill to **Old Dam**. At the junction in the hamlet, turn left back along **Church Lane** to complete the walk. ♦

Medieval hunting grounds

The Royal Forest of High Peak was once a vast hunting estate established by the Normans. Mostly open moor, the 'forest' still supported large numbers of deer, wild boar and wolves. It was administered from Peveril Castle at Castleton. A local court called the Swainmote, held where Chamber Farm now stands, could issue harsh fines and punishments for crimes such as encroaching on royal land, carrying a bow, and poaching.

Purple heather frames a gate on Eyam Moor

Eyam Moor

A walk of contrasts with a jaunt over open heather moor-land and along a secluded valley

What to expect:
Clear, often rugged paths; short section on quiet lane; steady final ascent

Distance/time: 7km/ 4½ miles. Allow 2¼ hours

Start: Junction of Sir William Hill Road with Edge Road, above Eyam

Grid ref: SK 224 780

Ordnance Survey Map: Explorer OL24 *Peak District: White Peak area: Buxton, Bakewell, Matlock & Dovedale*

After the Walk: Miner's Arms and tearooms in nearby Eyam

Walk outline

The walk begins across a rolling heather moor, which slopes toward the isolated clough of Bretton Brook. Dropping steeply into the main valley of Highlow Brook, the route undulates above the stream through scrub woodland, plantation and then pasture. Emerging on a narrow lane past the attractive seventeenth-century buildings of Hazelford Hall, the way climbs onto the hill for the final leg back across the moor.

Eyam Moor

Around 4,000 years ago, Britain's climate was warmer and drier than today. The uplands were ideal for farming and settlement, and subtle traces of ancient field systems, set-tlement and burial sites lie scattered across the moor. But as the Bronze Age progressed, wetter, colder conditions and overuse of the soil created the moorland heaths and bogs found today. Yet, despite their often bleak appearance, they provide valuable habitats for birds such as red grouse, golden plovers, hen harriers, curlews and short-eared owls. Ironically, global warming poses a threat to the moorland's ecology as the conditions that created them are reversed.

Hazelford Hall

Short-eared owl

The Walk

1. Leave over a stile at the junction of the track with the bend of the lane, not the nearby kissing-gate, and follow a path away beside the wall signed 'via Stoke Ford to Abney'.

Out to the right is Millstone Edge above Padley, while farther round are the parallel scarps of Froggatt and White edges. To the left, the heathery moor rises to Sir William Hill. The area has seen several Sir Williams. Sir William Saville was lord of the manor at the end of the 17th century when the turnpike road over the hill between Grindleford and Buxton was first constructed. Sir William Bagshawe, a royal physician to the Hanover royals, was born a century later. Finally, Sir William Cavendish, a Royalist who lived at Stoke Hall in the Derwent Valley and was the grandson of Bess of Hardwick. A resolute Elizabethan, Bess survived four marriages, collected three titles and became one of the richest women in the land. An astute business woman with interests in iron, glass and coal, she built both Chatsworth House and Hardwick Hall.

Beyond the boggy summit of **Eyam Moor**, the path falls in gradual descent towards the deep valley of **Bretton Clough**. The distant town is Hathersage above the Derwent Valley. The way later curves from the wall and eventually merges with another path to reach a gate and stile in the corner.

These open moors are the preferred habitat

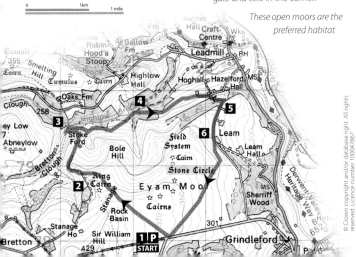

Gritsone guardian: *Above the confluence of Bretton Clough and Abney Clough*

of the short-eared owl. One of five owls making their home in Britain, short-eared owls have a larger world-wide distributions than almost any other bird. Preying on rodents and small birds, it commonly ranges over open moors, conifer plantations and coastal marshes.

With large, forward facing eyes and a round face it has a typically endearing 'owlish' look and can often been seen perching or slowly patrolling their territory in the fading light of late afternoon.

2. Continue downhill, the path gradually steepening before it winds into the scrub woodland above **Highlow Brook**. Towards the bottom, join another path and keep going down to a bridge across the stream at **Stoke Ford**.

Highlow is a name given to at least a couple of hills in the Peak; another lies near Monyash. Their names are not as contradictory as they seem. Low, like law *found in the northern borders and Scotland, is derived from an Old English word for hill, so High Low simply means High Hill.*

Heather and haze: *Swathes of purple heather stretch into the mist on Abney Low*

3. Remain on this bank and follow a path that undulates through the trees. The woodland later thins as the path crosses the gully of a side stream. Carry on over a stile beside a gate at the edge of the rising moor from which crystal **springs** seep water across the path, while the northern side of the valley is cloaked in conifer plantation. Accompany the left fence down to a gate, beyond which the path drops back into the trees.

4. A bridge takes the path over a side stream to a **bridge and ford** across the main flow. Again do not cross, instead negotiate a stile ahead and continue through a conifer plantation. Beyond the trees, carry on across pasture, passing through gates from field to field and then along a field track, which leads to **Hazelford Hall**. Keep going to emerge onto a lane at its end.

5. The climb up the steep lane is compensated by the views out across the valley. Keep going as the gradient shortly eases for some 800 metres/½ mile, until you reach an old barn above **Leam Hall**.

6. Leave the lane through a kissing-gate on the right and follow a clear path away to the left across the rising moor. Carry on through a gap in a wall higher up, the path eventually closing with a boundary on the left. The path continues at the edge of the moor, ultimately returning you to the track at the foot of **Sir William Hill** to complete the walk. ♦

Bees and heather

Late summer paints the moor a rich, regal purple as the heather comes into bloom. The heather flowers attract countless bees, giving a distinctive flavour to the honey, which is sometimes also used to make mead or beer. Bee keeping was integral to country life, and traditionally, when the bee keeper died, someone went to the hive to whisper the news. At Eyam, the bees were even given crumbs from the funeral meal.

Looking across the Derwent Valley from Curbar Edge

Big Moor

Combining impressive White, Curbar and Froggatt edges, this walk promises exhilarating views all the way

What to expect:

Good, clear moorland paths throughout with only moderate ascents

Distance/time: 9km/ 5½ miles. Allow 2½ hours

Start: Hay Wood National Trust pay and display car park

Grid ref: SK 255 777

Ordnance Survey Map: Explorer OL24 *Peak District: White Peak area: Buxton, Bakewell, Matlock & Dovedale*

After the Walk: The Grouse Inn at Longshaw, near Froggatt Edge

Walk outline

A short walk from the car park across fields leads to the main road and Grouse Inn. On the far side, the path rises through birch wood and heath onto the moor. Easy walking for the next 3km/2 miles takes the way along White Edge, passing a 'trig' column marking the highest point. Dipping across Sandyford Brook, the route cuts to the Curbar Gap, returning along the spectacular rim of Curbar and Froggatt edges.

The Derbyshire edges

Great sweeps of millstone grit border the White Peak's limestone plateau. Tilted back to the east by uplift, faulting and erosion has created long, westward facing escarpments, known locally as edges. They are dramatic features in an otherwise stark landscape.

Above the eastern bank of the River Derwent, the scarp rises in two parallel lines of cliff. White Edge is the higher, and although less dramatic, marks the apex of the moor and gives far-reaching views in all directions. Below, but rising more abruptly from the river valley, Curbar and Froggatt edges have spectacular cliffs and stacks that are a favourite haunt of rock climbers.

Summit of White Edge

Green hairstreak butterfly

The Walk

1. Begin behind the car park, following a path from it north (right) signed towards 'Jubilee Hill'. However, abandon it after 20 metres through a gate on the right. Cut the field corner to a second gate and head towards the far corner. Keep going in the same direction towards buildings, leaving over a stile onto the A625 by the **Grouse Inn**.

Walk past the pub, crossing to a path on the right just beyond. Head diagonally out towards a birch wood, passing through a gate in the corner. Turning right, continue through the trees. Reaching a junction in front of a rocky outcrop, bear right. Signed to 'White Edge', the path climbs around the bluff to carry on beside a wall at the edge of the moor.

2. After 400 metres/¼ mile, you meet a crossing path on the crest of the hill. Turn right through a gate and follow the gently rising line of **White Edge** towards Curbar Gap.

Although less craggy than many Derbyshire edges, the elevation of White Edge gives an extensive panorama across

the Derwent Valley towards the moors of Eyam and Longstone, while to the north the distinctive outcrops of Carl Wark and Higger Tor can be seen.

Despite the moor's apparent emptiness, wildlife is surprisingly abundant. Besides the many birds, a herd of roe deer roams the hill and in spring and summer you might come across common lizards or adders basking on a rock.

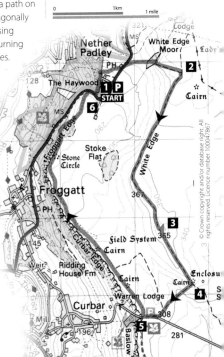

Rock stack: *The angular gritstone Pinnacle Rock high on Curbar Edge*

Look out, too, for an inscribed cube of stone beside the path, part of an art project inspired by the ancient guide stoops.

3. The Ordnance Survey 'trig' column marking the moor's highest point is set back from the path. Once you've visited it, return to the edge and continue along the main path, the ground gently falling as the scarp loses prominence.

There are over 6,500 triangulation, or 'trig', points dotted around Britain, erected by the Ordnance Survey from 1935 onwards during the re-triangulation of the country. They were strategically placed to be in direct line of sight of at least two other stations. Embedded on the top of each is a brass mount to carry a theodolite, which was then used to determine accurate angular measurements of neighbouring 'trigs'. Trigonometric calculation allowed the position of each to be determined with reference to a base line for map production.

Although generally placed on the summits of hills and mountains, on low

Golden hour: *A late evening light catches the weather-worn rocks on Curbar Edge*

lying ground any prominence might be employed. The lowest, in Norfolk, stands one metre below sea level. Today, aerial surveys and GPS have largely obviated their original purpose, but they remain a useful reference for walkers, particularly in remote and otherwise featureless areas.

4. Reaching a wall corner by a signpost, turn right to **Curbar Gap**. Descend to cross **Sandyford Brook**, rising beyond to leave the moor beside the **Curbar Gap car park**.

5. Cut across the car park to steps, from which a path is signed to 'Curbar Edge'. Follow it left and then right, joining a broader path that rises to a gate. A broad track leads away, set back from the lip of **Curbar Edge**.

However, the best views are from an informal path along the rim, but exercise care, particularly on windy days, for the drop is sheer.

After 1.5 kilometres/1 mile, the cliff swings to the north east, now sharing its name with the village below, **Froggatt**. Eventually the cliffs on **Froggatt Edge** subside and the path delves into woodland, later passing through a gate.

Nevertheless, there are still fine viewpoints, one almost at the end, where a large craggy boulder looks out over Nether Padley towards Hathersage.

6. Ultimately dropping out to the main road, walk ahead, crossing to leave by a gate on the left. A stepped path descends to a stream before climbing into the trees beyond. Head for the car park, just to the right, to finish. ♦

Moorland adders

The adder is Britain's only venomous snake, and is relatively common on moors and heaths, where it basks on rocks in a warm sun. Although a reptile, it gives birth to live young, which appear in late August. Adders hunt small mammals, lizards and frogs and will even take chicks from a nest. Using their venom to kill their prey, like all snakes they will then swallow it whole.

Looking towards Shutlingsloe from the summit of Shining Tor

Shining Tor

A straightforward but lengthy climb to the highest point on the Cheshire—Derbyshire border

What to expect:
Rough but clear moor-land paths and tracks; long, steady climb to the summit

Distance/time: 10km/ 6½ miles. Allow 3 hours

Start: Errwood Hall car park

Grid ref: SK 012 748

Ordnance Survey Map: Explorer OL24 *Peak District: White Peak area: Buxton, Bakewell, Matlock & Dovedale*

After the Walk: Cat and Fiddle at the summit of the A537 Buxton-Macclesfield road

Walk outline

From the Errwood Reservoir, the route climbs through woodland to Errwood Hall, continuing across the more open ground flanking Foxlow Edge. A short stretch of lane completes the climb to the ridge, where a path then undulates over Cats Tor to the summit. After dropping across the head of Shooter's Clough, an old packhorse trail descends towards the Goyt Valley. However, this is soon abandoned in favour of the wooded clough, providing a pretty finale to the walk.

Shining Tor

Shining Tor marks the highest point on the border between Cheshire and Derbyshire and is Cheshire's highest point. Although dropping east to elevated, rolling moorland that interrupts extensive views, the western face falls as a steep scarp overlooking the Cheshire Plain. The most dramatic sight is the distinctive summit of Shutlingsloe to the south, while on a clear day the Welsh Hills as far as Snowdon can be seen. Closer to is the giant radio telescope of Jodrell Bank, while to the north beyond Manchester the transmitter masts on Winter Hill can just be made out.

The Chapel

Golden plover

The Walk

1. An information board behind the car park marks the start of a path that rises away from the **Goyt Valley** and its reservoirs across open ground.

The River Goyt is a tributary of the Mersey and has its source on Axe Edge Moor, but the demand for water led Stockport Corporation to acquire the upper valley for the construction of reservoirs. Fernilee was the first to be completed in 1938, with Errwood opening 29 years later. They supply some 8 million gallons a day as well as providing a well-used resource for fishermen and yachters.

Passing through a gap in the top wall, walk forward to a broad track and follow it right through a barrier towards Errwood Hall. The track winds through a tangle of woodland along the side of a deep clough, shortly climbing to a junction.

The extensive forests around the reservoirs' catchment area help preserve the purity of the water draining into the lakes. Once controversial, they have long since become an accepted feature of the landscape. Much of the surrounding moorland and clough has been designated a Site of Special Scientific Interest to protect birds such as golden plovers, ring ouzels and goshawks.

2. Double back to the right to pass below the ruin of **Errwood Hall**. Narrowing beyond to a path, the way

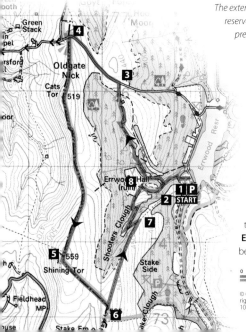

0   1km

1 mile

Blue and gold: *The flanks of Shining Tor lead the eye to Shutlingsloe's iconic conical peak*

descends, emerging from the trees to cross a stream. Walk on to a junction by a second bridge, but instead of crossing, turn right up steps to another junction and go left in the direction of Pym Chair. The path rises steadily across the open flank of **Foxlow Edge**, later passing above a small, circular **'chapel' or shrine**.

The Grimshawes of Errwood Hall were ardent travellers and returned from one of their trips accompanied by Dolores de Ybarguen, a Spanish noblewoman who *settled at the hall as governess and teacher at the local school. When she died, the circular, stone-built shrine was built in her memory.*

Carry on along the path, keeping left at a fork to emerge onto a lane.

3. Turning up the hill, the tarmac can be avoided by following a parallel path on the right.

4. Just before the crest of the hill, leave the lane by either of two gates on the left. Walk up to the wall, beside which a path heads away along the crest of the

Curves and colours: *Summer clouds echo the shape of the land below Shining Tor*

ridge. After the intermediate top of **Cats Tor**, the way rises clear to the **summit of Shining Tor**.

The 'trig' column lies on the other side of the wall, beyond which there is a fine view from the top of the crag across the Cheshire Plain and south to the distinctive peak of Shutlingsloe.

5. Return through the gate to the path and follow it down to the head of **Shooter's Clough**. Gaining height, pass through a gate at the top onto a crossing track.

These moors support breeding golden plovers. Although classed as waders, they migrate from lowland pastures to breed on upland heaths. Creating a shallow scrape amongst the vegetation, the female lays four eggs, feeding the young on worms and small insects.

6. Go left, walking steadily downhill towards the reservoir in the **Goyt Valley** below.

7. After 1 kilometre/¾ mile, turn through a gate in the left wall. A broad path descends back into the deep wooded valley of **Shooter's Clough**, winding through lazy zigzags to cross a stream at

the bottom. Now heading downstream, the trees are soon left behind, the path continuing to a T-junction with a track.

8. Turn right towards Errwood, keeping with the main trail and eventually reaching the junction at which you turned off to Errwood Hall earlier in the day. Keep ahead, retracing your outward steps to the car park to complete the walk. ♦

Errwood Hall

Built during the 1830s, Errwood Hall was the country residence of the Grimshawes, a wealthy Manchester family of merchant manufacturers. The estate extended over 2,000 acres and included farms, woodlands and even a coal mine. But when the family line died out around 1930, the hall was briefly used as a Youth Hostel and then demolished when the reservoir was built. Today, only atmospheric ruins remain.

Shutlingsloe's distinctive silhouette

Shutlingsloe

Although of modest height, Shutlingsloe is one of the most dramatic summits in the Peak

What to expect:
*Woodland trails, moorland paths, quiet lanes;
steep near summit, easy
scramble off*

Distance/time: 6km/ 3¾ miles. Allow 2 hours

Start: Clough House car park

Grid ref: SJ 987 698

Ordnance Survey Map: Explorer OL24 *Peak District: White Peak area: Buxton, Bakewell, Matlock & Dovedale*

After the Walk: Crag Inn, Wildboarclough

Walk outline

Beginning from Clough House car park, the walk follows the lane north to High Ash Farm. After cutting across fields, it rejoins the lane to the hilltop at Standing Stone. Track and path fringe Macclesfield Forest around the flank of Buxtors Hill to find a good path that strikes across the open moor to Shutlingsloe. From the summit an easy scramble drops to sloping pastures and a track, which doubles back past Banktop to the start.

Shutlingsloe

Despite its unpretentious height of only 506 metres, Shutlingsloe is the third highest hill in Cheshire and glories in being known as the 'Matterhorn of Cheshire'. The epithet derives from its distinctive conical profile when seen from the north.

On the one hand it overlooks the valley of Clough Brook, a tributary of the River Dane, and claims (like several other places) to have been the last refuge of the wild boar in England, while to the west its slopes fall to the former royal hunting estate of Macclesfield Forest.

Leaving the moor

Mountain hare

The Walk

1. Leave the car park at the entrance farthest from **Clough House Farm** and follow the lane right past a junction, up the valley for 1 kilometre/¾ mile.

The often-unpretentious stream of Clough Brook running beside the lane through the valley can sometimes turn visciously devastating, and some say that it is this 'wild bore' that gave the valley its name. Tragedy struck in May 1989 when a flash flood swept down the valley, destroying several bridges and sweeping away a car, instantly drowning its driver. The lane remained closed for more than six months while repairs were carried out.

2. Just after **High Ash Farm**, abandon it over a stile beside a gate on the left. A trod strikes out across the field towards a barn. Crossing an intermediate stile, pass left of the barn to find a gate onto the lane beyond. Walk up the hill to a junction.

3. Turn left along a gated track into **Macclesfield Forest**. Leave the track after 400 metres/¼ mile at a waypost. Bear left along a grass path, but keep ahead where it then forks to contour beside a wall across the flank of **Buxtors Hill**.

4. Dropping to meet another forest track, keep ahead, soon passing a bench judiciously sited to take advantage of a view through the trees to Tegg's Nose. A little farther along, felling has temporarily opened a wider panorama across the valley. After 400 metres/¼ mile, at the crest of the hill, branch left along a path that leads to a gate out of the trees.

On the up: *A clear, paved path heads across the peat moor towards Shutlingsloe*

5. Emerging onto **High Moor**, a sign points the way along a flagged path towards 'Shutlingsloe Farm' and 'Wildboarclough'.

Lucky walkers may see mountain hares around the hill. Unlike brown hares, which probably came to this country with the Romans, the mountain hare is native to Britain. Its bones have been found in southern England dating back more then 100,000 years. Habitat loss to grazing eventually confined its range to Scottish moors above 500 metres, but it has successfully been re-introduced to the Isle of Man and the Peak District.

Smaller than the brown hare and with shorter ears, it is nevertheless a sizeable mammal, clearly larger than a rabbit. Approaching winter brings on a moult in which the brown summer fur is replaced by a white coat, excellent camouflage for when the snow arrives. Although preferring grass, mountain hares will also forage upon heather and upland trees.

Green glow: *Shafts of sunlight spotlight drystone walled fields below Shutlingsloe*

Largely nocturnal, their presence is often betrayed in winter by tracks across a snowy hillside, while during summer they may occasionally be disturbed from their 'forms' hidden amongst the vegetation.

Broaching a rise, Shutlingsloe comes into view ahead, the path leading on to a kissing-gate. The ongoing route follows the wall to the right, crossing a stile before a final steep pull onto the **summit of Shutlingsloe**.

Sometimes written as Shuttlings Low, the hill's name derives from the Old English,
Scyttel's Hlaw, *meaning the hill of Scyttel, an otherwise forgotten local chieftain.*

6. The way off lies directly opposite and involves a short scramble down the abrupt eastern face of the crag, although this can be avoided by following the ridge a little way south before curving left down the hillside.

Below the crag, continue steeply down on a grass path, crossing a couple of stiles before finally meeting a tarmac track from **Shutlingsloe Farm**.

7. Follow it right down to a cattle-grid and there double back left on a gravel track to **Banktop**. After winding below the cottage, it continues in a long but

pleasant descent, ultimately finishing over a stile onto a lane.

8. The **Crag Inn** lies a short distance to the right, but the way back to the car park is across a **footbridge** spanning the river opposite. Walk up the field to a corner in front of a barn. Go left and then right through the farmyard to emerge onto a metalled track. The car park is then just to the left across a bridge, to complete the walk. ♦

Piggford Moor

Despite its wild appearance, heather moor is a man-made landscape. Even so, it is an important habitat for many wild birds, insects and small animals. Traditional management includes controlled grazing and rotational burning to regenerate the young plants on which many species feed, while predators such as foxes and crows are kept in check. As a result, golden plovers, short-eared owls, curlews and red grouse have all increased.

Useful Information

Visit Peak District & Derbyshire

The Peak's official tourism website covers everything from accommodation and special events to attractions and adventure. **www.visitpeakdistrict.com**

Peak District National Park

The Peak District National Park website also has information on things to see and do, plus a host of practical details to help you plan your visit. **www.peakdistrict.org**

Visitor Centres

The main Visitor Centres provide free information on everything from accommodation and transport to what's on and walking advice.

Bakewell	01629 816558	bakewell@peakdistrict.gov.uk
Castleton	01629 816572	castleton@peakdistrict.gov.uk
Moorland Centre, Edale	01433 670207	edale@peakdistrict.gov.uk
Upper Derwent	01433 650953	derwentinfo@peakdistrict.gov.uk
Marsden	01484 222555	marsden.visitorinformation@kirklees.gov.uk

Rail Travel

Four railway services cross the National Park:

The Hope Valley Line

The Derwent Valley Line

The Manchester to Buxton Line

The Manchester to Glossop Line

Information is available from National Rail Enquiries on 08457 484950 or: **www.nationalrail.com.uk**

Bus Travel

Peakland's towns and many of the villages are served by bus. For routes and timetables, call Traveline on: 0871 200 22 33 or visit: **www.traveline.info**

Weather

Online weather forecasts for the Peak District are available from the Met Office at: **www.metoffice.gov.uk/outdoor/mountainsafety/** and the Mountain Weather Information Service at: **www.mwis.org.uk/**